DISTANCE LEARNING

SPECIAL ISSUE: "AND FINALLY" COLUMNS

EDITOR
Michael Simonson
simsmich@nsu.nova.edu

MANAGING EDITOR
Charles Schlosser
cschloss@nsu.nova.edu

ASSISTANT EDITOR
Anymir Orellana
orellana@nsu.nova.edu

EDITORIAL ASSISTANT
Khitam Azaiza
azaiza@nova.edu

ASSOCIATION EDITOR
John G. Flores
jflores@usdla.org

PUBLISHER
Information Age Publishing
11600 North Community
    House Road, Ste. 250
Charlotte, NC 28277
(704) 752-9125
(704) 752-9113 Fax
www.infoagepub.com

ADVERTISING
United States Distance
    Learning Association
76 Canal Street, Suite 400

Boston MA 02114
800-275-5162 x11

EDITORIAL OFFICES
Fischler School of Education
    and Human Services
Nova Southeastern
    University
1750 NE 167th St.
North Miami Beach, FL
    33162
954-262-8563
FAX 954-262-3905
simsmich@nova.edu

PURPOSE

Distance Learning, an official publication of the United States Distance Learning Association (USDLA), is sponsored by the USDLA, by the Fischler School of Education and Human Services at Nova Southeastern University, and by Information Age Publishing. Distance Learning is published four times a year for leaders, practitioners, and decision makers in the fields of distance learning, e-learning, telecommunications, and related areas. It is a professional magazine with information for those who provide instruction to all types of learners, of all ages, using telecommunications technologies of all types. Articles are written by practitioners for practitioners with the intent of providing usable information and ideas for readers. Articles are accepted from authors with interesting and important information about the effective practice of distance teaching and learning.

SPONSORS

The United States Distance Learning (USDLA) is the professional organization for those involved in distance teaching and learning. USDLA is committed to being the leading distance learning association in the United States. USDLA serves the needs of the distance learning community by providing advocacy, information, networking and opportunity. www.usdla.org

The Fischler School of Education and Human Services (FSEHS) of Nova Southeastern University is dedicated to the enhancement and continuing support of teachers, administrators, trainers and others working in related helping professions throughout the world. The school fulfills its commitment to the advancement of education by serving as a resource for practitioners and by supporting them in their professional self development. The school offers alternative delivery systems that are adaptable to practitioners' work schedules and locations. School programs anticipate and reflect the needs of practitioners to become more effective in their current positions, to fill emerging roles in the education and related fields, and to be prepared to accept changing responsibilities within their own organizations.
FSEHS—NSU
1750 NE 167th St.
North Miami Beach, FL 33162
800-986-3223
www.schoolofed.nova.edu

INFORMATION AGE PUBLISHING
11600 North Community
House Road, Ste. 250
Charlotte, NC 28277
(704) 752-9125
(704) 752-9113 Fax
www.infoagepub.com

SUBSCRIPTIONS
Members of the United States Distance Learning Association receive *Distance Learning* as part of their membership. Others may subscribe to *Distance Learning*.
Individual Subscription: $60
Institutional Subscription: $150
Student Subscription: $40

DISTANCE LEARNING **RESOURCE INFORMATION:**
Visit http://www.usdla.org/html/resources/dlmag/index.htm

Advertising Rates and Information:
800-275-5162, x11

Subscription Information: Contact USDLA at
800-275-5162
info@usdla.org

DISTANCE LEARNING is indexed by the Blended, Online Learning and Distance Education (BOLDE) research bank.

DISTANCE LEARNING MAGAZINE
SPONSORED BY THE U.S. DISTANCE LEARNING ASSOCIATION
FISCHLER SCHOOL OF EDUCATION, NOVA SOUTHEASTERN UNIVERSITY
AND INFORMATION AGE PUBLISHING

MANUSCRIPT PREPARATION GUIDELINES

Distance Learning is for leaders, practitioners, and decision makers in the fields of distance learning, e-learning, telecommunications, and related areas. It is a professional journal with applicable information for those involved in providing instruction of all kinds to learners of all ages using telecommunications technologies of all types. Articles are written by practitioners for practitioners with the intent of providing usable information and ideas. Articles are accepted from authors with interesting and important information about the effective practice of distance teaching and learning. No page costs are charged authors, nor are stipends paid. Two copies of the issue with the author's article will be provided. Reprints will also be available.

1. Your manuscript should be written in Microsoft Word. Save it as a .doc file and also as a .rtf file. Send both versions on a CD or flash drive.

2. *Single* space the entire manuscript. Use 12 point Times New Roman (TNR) font.

3. Laser print your paper.

4. Margins: 1" on all sides.

5. Do not use any page numbers, or embedded commands. Documents that have embedded commands, including headers and footers, will be returned to the author.

6. Include a cover sheet with the paper's title and with the names, affiliations and addresses, telephone, and e-mail for all authors.

7. Submit the paper on a flash drive that is clearly marked. The name of the manuscript file should reference the author. In addition, submit two paper copies. A high resolution .jpg photograph of each author is required. Send the flash drive and paper copies to: Michael R. Simonson

Editor
Distance Learning
Instructional Technology and
Distance Education
Nova Southeastern University

Fischler School of Education and
Human Services
1750 NE 167th Street
North Miami Beach, FL 33162
simsmich@nova.edu
(954) 262-8563

The Manuscript

To ensure uniformity of the printed proceedings, authors should follow these guidelines when preparing manuscripts for submission. DO NOT EMBED INFORMATION. YOUR PAPER WILL BE RETURNED IF IT CONTAINS EMBEDDED COMMANDS OR UNUSUAL FORMATTING INFORMATION.

Word Processor Format
Manuscripts should be written in Microsoft Word.

Length
The maximum length of the body of the paper should be about 3000 words.

Layout
Top and bottom margins: 1.0"
Left and right margins: 1.0"

Text
Regular text: 12 point TNR, left justified
Paper title: 14 point TNR, centered
Author listing: 12 point TNR, centered
Section headings: 12 point TNR, centered
Section sub-heading: 12 point TNR, left justified

Do not type section headings or titles in all-caps, only capitalize the first letter in each word. All type should be single-spaced. Allow one line of space before and after each heading. Indent, 0.5", the first sentence of each paragraph.

Figures and Tables
Figures and tables should fit width 6½" and be incorporated into the document.

Page Numbering
Do not include or refer to any page numbers in your manuscript.

Graphics
We encourage you to use visuals—pictures, graphics, and charts—to help explain your article. Graphics images (.jpg) should be included at the end of your paper.

IN UPCOMING ISSUES

Introduction to the Special Issue

Michael Simonson

When examining the last dozen years of *Distance Learning*, it is apparent that the field of distance education has evolved—emerged in education as something real, vibrant, and growing—maybe matured. Distance education is now widely accepted, even if often misunderstood. Keywords used in *Distance Learning* such as skeuomorph, virtual design, and accreditation have been replaced in more recent issues by words such ethics, colonialism, and bookicide.

What has happened to the field? Obviously, distance education, e-learning, and virtual schooling have matured. It is now common to see advertising on TV, hear speakers at conferences, and read articles in local newspapers about the field. And, it unfortunately is also common to hear about fraud, ethical violations, malpractice, and the end of books as side effects of the growth of distance education. Perhaps distance education has not matured into adulthood, but is still in its adolescence.

Are the problems with distance education "bad" or typical? Probably both. This issue of *Distance Learning* looks back over the last decade and reintroduces significant issues, most of which remain important, and concentrates collections of "And Finally" columns on issues that need additional emphasis. Three sections and 24 topics are included in this issue of *Distance Learning* journal. Enjoy!

Michael Simonson, Editor, *Distance Learning*, and Program Professor, Programs in Instructional Technology and Distance Education, Fischler School of Education, Nova Southeastern University, 1750 NE 167 St., North Miami Beach, FL 33162. Telephone: (954) 262-8563. E-mail: simsmich@nsu.nova.edu

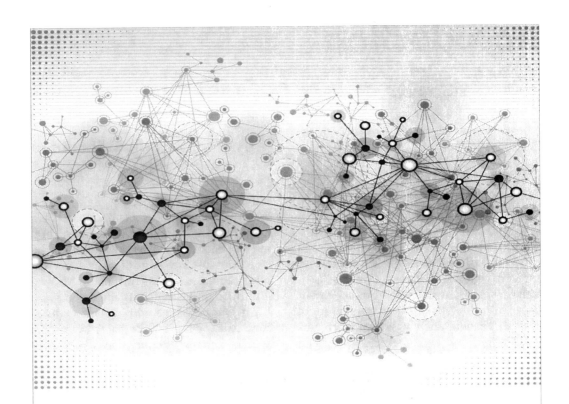

TEACHING AND LEARNING AT A DISTANCE

Foundations of Distance Education

SIXTH EDITION

Michael Simonson

Sharon Smaldino

Susan Zvacek

Get Your Copy Today—Information Age Publishing

Teacher as Skeuomorph. Teacher as What?

Michael Simonson

John Howells' new book, *Management of Innovation and Technology* (2005) is not the easiest book to read. It is however, quite interesting. In the first chapter, he discusses skeuomorphs. A skeuomorph, in case you have forgotten, is an element of design that has lost its original function but is nevertheless retained. An example is the square on top of a Doric Column. Originally, columns were made of

Michael Simonson, Editor, *Distance Learning*, and Program Professor, Programs in Instructional Technology and Distance Education, Fischler School of Education, Nova Southeastern University, 1750 NE 167 St., North Miami Beach, FL 33162. Telephone: (954) 262-8563. E-mail: simsmich@nsu.nova.edu

wood, so they were topped with a wooden square to distribute the stress. Marble and stone columns did not require this square but, for esthetic purposes, it was retained, thus becoming a skeuomorph. Other examples are watch pockets on jeans, plastic dinnerware made to look like stoneware (including the imperfections), and the consumer version of the Hummer, made to look like the original, but certainly not ready for the next war.

In distance education, especially online instruction that is asynchronous, the role of the teacher is significantly different, even unrecognizable when compared to traditional classroom instruction. In classrooms, teachers present information, talk, draw on the board, demonstrate, and take apart; they do it all. The classroom teacher has a critical and necessary role. Without the teacher in the traditional classroom, teaching and learning—education—would not occur.

Conversely, in an asynchronous, online course the instructor does none of these traditional things. True, many of our instructional tools allow us to simulate the classroom and the functions of the classroom teacher, but it is not the same.

We have kept the teacher, but is the teacher's function really critical? If we look at the teacher's changing role superficially, as some do, one might conclude that teachers have no real purpose anymore; they are skeuomorphs.

Admittedly, the word is a little hard to deal with, but then so is the idea that teachers have lost their original function. However, if we are realistic, we recognize that teachers are becoming designers, organizers, motivators, and assessors, among other things; roles that teachers have long been advocating as vital to the education process, even more important than presenting.

And finally, recognizing that teaching as we have known it is losing its original function is an important—albeit first— step. As distance education leaders, we can take an important, positive role in identifying the new teacher.

REFERENCE

Howells, J. (2005). *The management of innovation and technology.* London: SAGE.

TEACHERS ARE BECOMING DESIGNERS, ORGANIZERS, MOTIVATORS, AND ASSESSORS.

Online Instruction— The Seven Virtues

Or, How to Avoid the Seven Deadly Presentation Sins

Michael Simonson

L uck and mystery have long been associated with the number seven. Seven is a prime number. It is the most important number in dice games. There are 7 days in a week. There were 7 years of plenty and 7 years of famine. Who can forget the Magnificent Seven? And, there are seven deadly sins that are balanced by seven virtues. The seven virtues are humility, charity, patience, diligence, kindness, temperance, and chastity. Centuries ago, these seven virtues were proposed to help people avoid the seven deadly sins.

When it comes to education and online teaching, seven is an important number. It takes seven years to get tenure, seven is the number of classes normally taught in a year, and there are seven best practices of the online instructor. We could call these practices virtues, and apply them as ways to avoid the seven deadly presentation sins often seen in classrooms, webinars, and videoconferences.

Humility is the first of the seven virtues and is the virtue that counters the sin of pride. For the distance educator, humility means *avoiding the talking head*. In other words, when presenting in a webinar or videoconference the person doing the presenting should not dominate the screen, the monitor, or the podium. Certainly, the speaker should establish themselves, but quickly more relevant visual information should be shown—graphics, visuals, definitions, and examples.

Charity is the virtue that counters the sin of greed. When teaching online, charity means *keep the length appropriate*. Sometimes presenters think that their topic is so important and complex that they "overpresent." To minimize the tendency to run-on in a lesson, the class should be organized around single concepts. The single concept is the building block of effective instruction. The single concept is easily presented in 3-5 minutes with a strong introduction to the concept, an explanation with examples of the concept, and a summary statement that clarifies how this concept fits with others.

Patience is the virtue that is the opposite of the sin of wrath. In online teaching the instructor needs to *plan for interaction*. Expecting students to interact automatically, without prompting, is foolhardy.

Instead of being disappointed, even wrathful, if no one asks relevant questions, the online teacher should plan for interaction by seeding questions, using chat areas for small group discussions, and developing strategies that tease out interaction.

Diligence is the virtue that wards off the sin of sloth. For the distance educator, this means *preparing and planning*. No matter how many times a topic has been taught or hardware has been used, the need for careful planning and preparation are a must. Review the materials, test the equipment, and practice. A last minute arrival to the course management system or at the webinar site is sometimes unavoidable, but this should be the exception rather than standard practice.

Kindness is the virtue and envy is the sin. The online presenter should *design for the audience*, and plan presentations around what the audience wants and needs to know. Certainly, personal anecdotes are fun, and "war stories" can enliven a topic. However, these distractions might be amusing, but playing to the audience is best left for other performances, not online instruction.

Temperance is a goal and gluttony is to be avoided. The online instructor should have *presenting as the goal in order to avoid lecturing*. Talking is the easiest for most experienced teachers. Unfortunately, the lecture is often the poorest way to promote an understanding in students. Rather, it is best to present, based on a careful design while using visuals that support the topic.

Chastity, yes chastity, is the final virtue that is the counter to the sin of lust. It is important to examine the intent of the organization that is offering online instruction. This institution *must be above reproach*. If the phrases "return on investment," or "cost effectiveness" become the primary reasons why distance education is offered, then the sin of institutional lust may be evident. Chastity also implies *purity*. For the distance educator, intentions are critical. Teaching at a distance is a way to promote learning through the appropriate use of instructional and communication technologies. The dedication to high-quality materials, rigorous instructional standards, and uniform expectations are necessary if distance education generally, and live, online instruction specifically, are to be considered as equivalent alternatives and partners of more traditional approaches to teaching and learning.

And finally, Renaissance philosophers thought that great personal efforts and external enforcement would be required to help the common person avoid the seven deadly sins. To help, the seven virtues were identified. Today, great personal effort applying best practices is needed by distance educators. We do not want external enforcement. Let's be virtuous!

Designing the "Perfect" Online Course

Michael Simonson

ictionary definitions of the word *perfect* are universally similar: without defect, faultless. Certainly it is foolish to try to quickly define the perfect online course; a course without defect and faultless. However, with the current "rush to go online," many instructional designers, distance educators, and training directors and being asked to design just such a course—an effective, rigorous, yet interesting online course—a "perfect" online course.

So, for the sake of the naiveté of those asking and the motivation of many distance educators to want to help, let us examine what the best practices literature seems to be indicating about online courses—good, if not perfect ones—and make a recommendation. (Actually, the components of an online course summarized in this column are derived from the recent edition of *Teaching and Learning at a Distance: Foundations of Distance Education.*)

When designing an online course, there are three organizational categories to consider: course structure, course contents, and artifacts of learning. It might also be informative to look at the organization of the major subdivision of a typical online course: the course unit.

COURSE STRUCTURE

The typical college course is a three-semester, 15-week course with a title something like "Management of Service Centers," or "Introduction to Educational Statistics." Certainly most educators know that a three-credit college course will meet about three times a week for the 15 weeks of the semester, or for about 45 class sessions.

And, for every hour a student is in class he or she should expect to spend about 2 hours outside of class preparing, reading, or studying, for a semester total of somewhere between 100 and 140 hours.

What about a class that does not have class session—an online class? If the course designer applies the same logic to an online class as to a traditional class, then, in an online course an average student should expect:

- Between 100 and 140 hours of "work "during the semester, or about 7-9 hours per week. This time would be spent reading, studying, writing, posting, viewing, listening, and chatting.
- A course that is organized around 3 major units, each with about 5 modules. Modules would be studied for about a week.

And, the instructor should also expect to devote between 100 and 140 hours of effort, organizing, posting, reading, grading, and interacting, or between 7-9 hours per week.

COURSE CONTENT

Effective online courses emphasize instructional content that presents in a variety of ways what students should learn. The key organizational document for the online course is the syllabus that gives most, if not all, the important information about the course content and organization. The syllabus contains the sequence of topics, course objectives, assignments, rubrics, reading and viewing lists, and other information needed by the student to "keep up and stay informed."

Additionally, the perfect online course would use a course management system. It is hard to imagine an online course, especially a "perfect" one, without a course management system. The course management system would be a meeting place, a virtual classroom, and the venue where instruction and learning interact.

Next, the online course must have a considerable amount of instructor involvement—even presentations, although lecturing by the instructor of the online course is probably not conducive to perfection. The instructor should introduce himself or herself distribute periodic and regular organizational e-mails, personally contact individual students, make postings to threaded discussion, participate in chats, both spoken and typed, and make short and on-target presentations—single concept lectures.

Textbooks and other reading materials remain the mainstay for delivering content in most courses, including the online course. The average for a typical online course is 2-3 textbooks. The modern, well-chosen textbook can provide the content information for most courses.

Finally, the online course should have single-concept videos, audio explanations or descriptions, narrated visuals and other multimedia content. Also of importance are the contents of the virtual portion of the course—chats and threaded discussions, for example—that are built and constructed during the course.

ARTIFACTS OF LEARNING

Some would probably choose a different phrase than "artifacts of learning," but most who study online education look for observable objects, things, and artifacts that are evidence of student learning. A comprehensive investigation of online courses yields the following general set of expectations for student assignments:

- Three major graded assignments, usually one for each major unit of the course. These major assignments can be exams, problem/scenario solutions, research papers, group projects, or media productions.
- Approximately 10 minor graded assignments, such as discussion postings, chat participations, e-mails, wiki input, or blog postings.

These artifacts, or learning outcomes, are at the core of the perfect online course (and at the heart of almost any course, as instructional designers often tell us).

If the typical course is examined in more detail, and the major building block of the course—the unit—is examined, its organization might look like this:

- A video introduction to the unit produced by the instructor that in 5 minutes or less explains what this unit is "all about."
- An audio explanation of the major assignment for this unit, made by the instructor and posted online as an audio file; this explanation would supplement the syllabus explanation and would be what students are referred to when they ask "what am I supposed to do?" Obviously, the assignment rubric would be explained in this "podcast."
- A reading assignment of several hundred pages from one or more of the course textbooks, or a series of readings from the Web or from a course packet.

- A few short video viewings that highlight key ideas or that demonstrate important processes.
- A series of threaded discussion questions that build on one another to provide a sequenced construction of information that supports the unit's final assignment. Instructors are actively involved in discussions early in the unit, but reduce their involvement as students begin to grasp the content more completely.
- Chats, mostly between students working as individuals or in teams, in which between-student interaction is stressed. Instructors monitor chats, but are not overly involved.
- A few instructor presentations, either prerecorded or presented live using voice-over-Internet technologies.

This typical unit would last about 5 weeks, and would build on previous units of study and contribute to subsequent units. The three units in a typical online course would be the "three-legged stool" supporting the overall purpose of the course.

And finally, let us not kid ourselves; the perfect online course is a pipe dream—according to the dictionary again, a pipe dream is the result one gets from smoking one of those funny pipes, so let us be more realistic (and legal). The key to an effective course is the direct, purposeful involvement of a knowledgeable teacher; one with content knowledge, teaching skills, and design experience.

REFERENCE

Simonson, M., Smaldino, S., Albright, M., & Zvacek, S. (2009). *Teaching and learning at a distance: Foundations of distance education* (4th ed.). Boston, MA: Pearson.

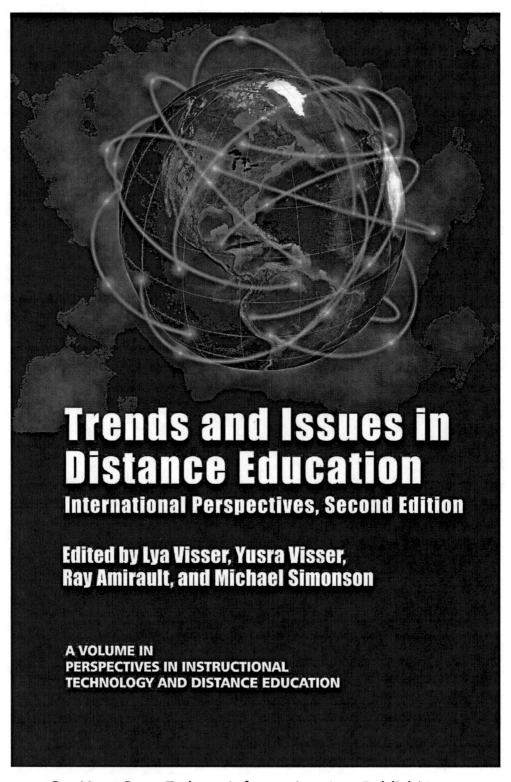

Trends and Issues in Distance Education

International Perspectives, Second Edition

Edited by Lya Visser, Yusra Visser,
Ray Amirault, and Michael Simonson

A VOLUME IN
PERSPECTIVES IN INSTRUCTIONAL
TECHNOLOGY AND DISTANCE EDUCATION

Get Your Copy Today—Information Age Publishing

Design
The Fundamental Element

Michael Simonson

On October 25, 1965, downtown St. Louis stopped in its tracks and thousands watched as the last piece of the mammoth Gateway Arch was being put into place. The weight of the two sides required braces to prevent them from falling against each other. Fire hoses poured water down the sides to keep the stainless steel cool, which kept the metal from expanding as the sun rose higher. Some horizontal adjustments were required, but when the last piece was put into place and the braces released, it fit perfectly, according to plan, and no one was surprised (Liggett, 1998). The thousands of onlookers applauded as the sun reflected off the bright span. The architects and engineers who were also watching smiled and went back to their offices.

Just like the Arch, distance education requires a careful process that includes systematic design before implementation. Success is almost guaranteed if all the pieces of the plan receive the same attention as the most obvious. The base sections of the Gateway Arch required more engineering savvy and study than any other component. The last and most visible span that connected the two halves received the most attention from the thousands of onlookers, but success was directly related to how the original supports were positioned.

Design is the fundamental element of effective instruction. Many think that the traditional systematic models of instructional design are not relevant to online teaching. Some claim that the traditional models of design such as the Dick, Carey, and Carey's model, and its derivative the ADDIE model, cannot be readily applied to instruction that is delivered to distant learners. Some claim that systematic planning is not important or even needed when learner-centered instruction is developed.

In spite of claims, the evidence remains clear that the key to effective instruction is the concept of design, defined by Seels and Richey (1994) as: "the process of specifying conditions for learning. The purpose of design is to create strategies and production at the macro level, such as programs and curricula, and at the micro level, such as lessons and modules" (p. 30).

At the root of most widely practiced and classic design approaches is the concept of systems. The idea of systems used in instruction is derived from Bertalanffy's General Systems Theory (1968), and Banathy's Instructional Systems (1968, 1991), usually called instructional systems design. This process has served as the intellectual technique of those in the field of instructional technology and distance education for decades.

Instructional designers, the engineers of quality instruction similar to the construction engineers and architects who designed the Gateway Arch, are on the front-lines of distance education implementation. Certainly, modern interpretations of the ADDIE model, such as the Unit-Model-Topic approach (Simonson, Smaldino, Albright, & Zvacek, 2012), have been proposed to clarify and simplify the approaches for the systematic design of distance delivered instruction. However, any approach that makes claims about quality but that does not have the systems approach at its foundation should be considered suspect.

And finally, Aeschylus once again provides insight about why an organization should be concerned about quality instruction delivered at a distance: "resolve is not to seem, but to be, the best."

REFERENCES

Banathy, B. (1991). *Systems design of education.* Englewood Cliffs, NJ: Educational Technology Publications.

Banathy, B. (1968). *Instructional systems.* Belmont, CA: Fearon.

Bertalanffy, L. (1968). *General systems theory.* New York, NY: Braziller.

Liggett, R. (1998). A prescription for telemedicine. *Telemedicine Today, 6*(5), 2.

Seels, B., & Richey, R. (1994). *Instructional technology: The definition and domains of the field.* Washington, DC: Association for Educational Communications and Technology.

Simonson, M., Smaldino, S., Albright, M., & Zvacek, S. (2012). *Teaching and learning at a distance: Foundations of distance education* (5th ed.). Boston, MA: Pearson.

DESIGN IS THE FUNDAMENTAL ELEMENT OF EFFECTIVE INSTRUCTION.

Designing the "Perfect" Online *Program*

Michael Simonson

"The Perfect Online Course" was described by Orellana, Hudgins, and Simonson (2009). This book of readings clearly presented issues central to course design such as time, organization, production, evaluation, and accreditation. It is an important planning document for the distance educator.

Since then, best practices for course design have become much more widely understood. However, Orellana, Hudgins and Simonson's book did not explain how to design the "perfect online *program*." Developing an entire program to be offered at a distance is considerably more complex than designing an online course.

Schools, universities, and organizations are moving quickly to offer classes, programs, and training at a distance. Most seem to be gradually making the transition from traditional offerings to distance education by first trying parts of classes, then individual courses, next blended courses, and finally entire distance-delivered programs.

Documenting the process of transitioning from traditional offerings to distance education has not been a priority of those involved in this process. It seems that "trial and error" is the favored approach, rather than a more reasoned process supported by applied research. There are some guides available, if not all in one location. For example in 2005, Simonson wrote about the eight steps for transforming an organization, with the primary purpose of the transformation being the move to distance delivered offerings. And, in 2012, the development of distance education policy and plans was described. What is missing is a combination of the two approaches—the process of distance education implementation and the artifacts needed to support the move. Certainly, research is needed in this area.

At this point it has become clear that the following two components are needed when an organization plans to infuse distance education as a mission-central approach:

1. First, an academic technology/distance education plan is needed. This plan includes the following components:

   - vision statement;
   - mission statement;
   - guiding principles;
   - definitions;
   - goals;
   - policy development processes;
   - timeline;
   - policy review and faculty guidance;
   - references; and
   - resources.

2. Next, a process for diffusion and implementation of distance education

is needed. This process includes these components:

- development of a sense of urgency by the organization's leaders;
- identification and empowerment of a powerful planning group;
- identification of a clear, widely understood and agreed-on vision
- identification of those willing to act on the vision;
- development of plans to guarantee short term successes—successes that are widely publicized;
- agreement on the process to combine successes; and
- development and adoption of successes into models for additional implementation.

At the heart of the plan and process is the role of stakeholders, especially teachers, professors, and trainers. Certainly, leaders can and must support the transformation process, but those expected to implement changes—the teachers, professors, and trainers—are the groups who will promote or limit success.

The ingredients of a successful, distance delivered academic program include:

- committed and strong organizational leader;
- assessment and statement of need;
- technology plan with a detailed program for implementation of distance education;
- steering committee led by faculty that includes stakeholders such as students, staff, administrators, and alumni;

- detailed timeline;
- formative and summative evaluation plan;
- course design model, such as the unit-module-topic approach;
- full-time faculty person to implement the plan;
- instructional designer with media production skills;
- provision for a help desk for students and faculty;
- distance education policy manual for use by students, faculty, and most important, support staff;
- course management system and media production facilities and equipment;
- templates for syllabi and course components;
- budget.

And finally, it is important not to be overly worried about the many small decisions that must be made, for as Thoreau said, "Our life is frittered away by detail … simplify, simplify."

REFERENCES

Orellana, A., Hudgins, T. L., & Simonson, M. (Eds.). (2009). *The perfect online course.* Charlotte, NC: Information Age.

Simonson, M. (2005). Distance education: Eight steps for transforming an organization. *Quarterly Review of Distance Education, 6*(2), vii-viii.

Simonson, M., & Schlosser, C. (2012). Institutional policy issues. In M. Moore (Ed.), *Handbook of distance education* (3rd ed.). Mahwah, NJ: Erlbaum.

Rules of Thumb, or DeRoTs

Michael Simonson

We all have heard of the phrase "rule of thumb," or "rules of thumb." Generally, this means a widely applicable process that is often used, even if it is not always.

It is often fun to try to find out where phrases like "rule of thumb" come from. In today's world, if a person wants to find something out, they often "Google it." (Do you suppose in 100 years someone will write about googling and wonder where that funny word came from?).

At any rate, if you Google "rule of thumb" you will find there are many explanations about where the phrase came from—everything from violence (proper thickness of a stick used to discipline someone or something), to physical measurement (distance between the base of the thumbnail and the first joint is an inch), to wind measurement (raising a wet thumb into the air), or to setting a table (in order set a row of plates one places the thumb on the edge of the table and extends it).

My personal favorite is how brewers use of "rule of thumb." For makers of Pete's Wicked Ale, the phrase was attributed to the practice of dipping a thumb in the ale to determine if the beer wort had cooled to the proper temperature for adding yeast.

Distance education is beginning to develop its "rules of thumb," also. It may be a sign that not enough research is being conducted in the field—but still, rules of thumb do have a certain amount of value

when decisions need to be made. Several DeRoTs are being applied by distance educators. (A DeRoT is a Distance Education Rule of Thumb.)

- DeRoT 1: One instructor can be responsible for 2-4 distance-delivered courses at a time.
- DeRoT 2: A full-time student can successfully participate in 4-6 online courses at one time. On the other hand, students working full-time should not enroll in more than 2, possibly 3 online courses at one time.
- DeRoT 3: A three-credit college course, taught at a distance should require students to commit about 8-10 hours per week during a 15-week term.
- DeRoT 4: Instructors facilitating threaded discussions should make about 1 posting for every 4 student postings early in a course and gradually reduce postings to about 1 in 10 near the end of the course, as students take on more responsibility for their own learning.
- DeRoT 5: Threaded discussions, when graded, are valued more highly by students. A student should make at a minimum at least three postings for each threaded discussion question—one in direct response to the question, one posting in response to another student's posting, and one in response to what

other students have posted in order to build a thread.

- DeRoT 6: One instructor, working alone teaching an online class, should have about 20 students, give or take five (actually, this rule of thumb is supported by research reported by Anymir Orellana in volume 7, issue 3 of the *Quarterly Review of Distance Education*).

Send us your DROTs; certainly there are others. Then, let us get someone to conduct research to move from the rules of thumb practiced by crafts, to the research and theory supporting best practices used by professions.

And finally, an important "rule of thumb" for column writers is to keep it short!

RULES OF THUMB NEED TO BE VALIDATED BY RESEARCH.

Podcasting ... or "Seeds Floated Down From the Sky"

Michael Simonson

Bud-like seeds floated down from the sky—from space actually. They were not noticed at first, but soon the seeds grew into pods, plantlike oblong objects that when ripe disgorged a terrible creature, a creature that killed and eliminated humans and replaced them with exact physical replicas that were identical in appearance but lacking in any emotion. Podpeople.

This sentence could be the plot-line to one of the four motion pictures made over the last 50 years based on Jack Finney's 1955 book *The Body Snatchers*. The film most remember was released in 1979, starring Donald Sutherland, who was one of the last on earth to remain free of will and independent of the pod menace.

Another explanation of this sentence might be a teacher's lament about the students in class constantly putting the tiny "bugs" in their ears to listen to the tens of thousands of rap tunes on their personal iPod, hidden in a back-pack.

The iPod has become an icon in the first decade of the twenty-first century, and podcasting has become one of the most talked-about applications in distance education. Podcasting and iPods are written about in the popular press, in journals, and even in the prestigious *Chronicle of Higher Education*. The *Chronicle* recently published a long article with the unfortunate title "How to Podcast Campus Lectures."

Podcasting is not a new idea. It has been around at least since the audio tutorial movement and the Sony Walkman. A podcast is really a single concept event that is explained by an audio file, or an audio file supplemented by still pictures or video. The most widespread and current example of a type of a podcast is a song, usually 3 to 5 minutes long available in an electronic file format, such as MP3 or MP4, that also might be available as a music video with singers, dancers, and actors in addition to the song. Luther Vandross' tune "Always and Forever" is a wonderful 4-minuteand-54-second example. The tune is also available as a music video showing Van-dross singing the song.

Individual songs work well as podcasts because most modern tunes have the characteristics of an effective single concept event—what many now are calling a podcast, which really is a learning object that is stored in an .mpeg format. The characteristics of an *effective* podcast are as follows:

- A podcast is a single idea that can be explained verbally or, if necessary, with audio and appropriate still or motion pictures (not a face talking);
- A podcast is a recorded event that is 310 minutes long;
- A podcast is part of a series with each single event related to others;
- A podcast is a learning object available in an electronic format that is easily played, most often as an MP3 file;
- A podcast is stored on a Web site or other Internet location for easy access; and
- A podcast is current and changed or updated frequently.

In spite of what the *Chronicle* says, a recording of a lecture is a poor example of a podcast. Rather, it is best to "chunk" the class into five or six single concept blocks, each as a separate learning object. Effective lecturers do this already; they break up their class session into related topics. These topics can become podcasts when they are recorded electronically in an .mpeg file format, especially if they are supplemented with related examples and recorded in a proper location without distracting background noises. Podcasts are a reincarnation or reinvention of what the mastery learning movement of the 1960s called single concept files or single concept films. They were effective then, and can be effective today.

And finally, let's call them something other than podcasts. Mpegcast doesn't have the same cachet as podcast, but then Mpegcast doesn't remind everyone of Donald Sutherland pointing his finger at the last normal person, either.

REFERENCES

Read, B. (2007, January 26). How to podcast campus lectures. *Chronicle of Higher Education,* A32-A35.

Finney, J. (1955). *The body snatchers.* New York, NY: Dell.

Don't Tell Them
The Top 10 Tips for Student Success in Online Courses

Michael Simonson

This column is for online instructors only. If students get a copy of these 10 tips, they will know our secrets. On the other hand, it might be a good idea to share these 10 suggestions with everyone—just to keep things fair. These tips are ways to meet the challenge of being an isolated learner. They help students build a learning community—so they really are for students.

- **Tip 1:** Get to know your instructor and try to help him or her get to know you. An e-mail or even a short note mailed using the postal system is a good way to start. Send your introduction at the start of the term.
- **Tip 2:** Since discussions are a very popular tool used in most online courses, be one of the first to post in order to get your name at the top of the listing of student postings, and always, *always* read instructor posts and respond to them. Instructors like this.
- **Tip 3:** Be one of the last, if not *the* last, student to post. This puts your name at the end of the thread where it is very obvious to the instructor. This also gives you a chance to "have the last word."
- **Tip 4:** When synchronous online instruction is scheduled using Skype, Elluminate, or some other VoIP (voice over Internet protocol), be one of the first to sign in, as soon after the instructor signs in as you can; this way your name appears early when the instructor is paying attention to see who is participating.
- **Tip 5:** Get organized; the syllabus, semester schedule, and list of assignments are the most important documents that provide structure to an online course. Read and understand these documents. Instructors get annoyed if it seems that students have not read the syllabus or met assignment requirements.
- **Tip 6:** Anticipate! Be an attentive student, and be on time. But, fight the urge to be early. If you complete assignments early this may give your instructor the feeling that his or her teaching is not important. Certainly, never be late, but if you are, be sure to inform your instructor that you will complete the tardy assignment as soon as possible.
- **Tip 7:** Get to know your classmates: collaborate, cooperate, and meet (really or virtually). Offer to get together regularly to talk about assignments or to discuss tricky concepts; build your own learning community.

- **Tip 8:** Create an academic profile that includes a professional photograph and academic information. A little personal information is okay, but not too much; keep things professional.
- **Tip 9:** Never use social media for academic activities; social media such as Facebook are for personal, not professional activities. Meet classmates in Facebook, but do not friend your instructor; they want to be friendly, but not be friends.
- **Tip 10:** Never copy, never cut and paste, and always write in your own words. Use the old trick of *closed book* note taking. Read, then close the book or shut the computer, then take notes. If you want, return to the book or online resource to write an accurate citation and to check details, but do not be tempted to cut and paste; you will forget that you copied and the instructor will catch you!

And finally, online classes require a great deal of self-discipline. George Washington said, "Discipline is the soul of the army." For the online learner, discipline is the key to success. Remember, your professors want you to learn so they will prepare challenging courses. They also want to help you meet the challenge.

MOST IMPORTANT—ONLINE COURSES REQUIRE A GREAT DEAL OF SELF DISCIPLINE.

Will You Be My Friend?

Michael Simonson

We all know what it means to be a friend. We learn early in life that, as Emerson said, "the only way to have a friend is to be one." A friend is a person admired, respected, whose company is enjoyed. The idea of friends has recently changed, however, at least in social networking applications. According to Boyd and Ellison (2007), social networks are Web-based services that allow persons to construct a public or semipublic profile within a system, to articulate a list of other users with whom they share connections, and view and move through a list of links made by themselves and others. Most often these locations are called "social networking sites." Social network sites such as MySpace and Facebook have attracted millions of participants who blog, share messages, post photos and videos, and list their friends, all in personally constructed profiles.

To participate in a social network site a user constructs a profile and by this act the social networker becomes real in a virtual world. They "type oneself into being," as Suden (2003) stated. One characteristic of most social networking sites is the listing of friends; friending. Social networkers name those they want to list as friends, and in most cases the request to be a friend requires an affirmative response. Some sites even allow top eight or top 10 lists of friends; as Boyd (2006) said, "in a culture where it is socially awkward to reject someone's Friendship, ranking them provides endless drama and social awkwardness" (p. 11).

Many who study the phenomena of social networking refer to the idea of Web 2.0, a trend in the use of the Internet and Web that is based on collaboration and information sharing. Web 2.0 is not a new network, nor a thing. Web 2.0 is an idea in people's heads, based on the interaction between the user and provider. Examples are eBay, Wikipedia, Skype, and Craigslist.

So, what does this all mean to the distance educator? Certainly it is nice to have friends, even virtual ones, and social networks seem to have reached the point of "critical mass" and are here to stay, at least until a new innovative use of the Web evolves.

The importance of social networking makes the concept important to distance educators. At the least, a modest understanding of social networking is a must for distance educators. And, it is likely that more depth of understanding will be needed. The taxonomy of social networking for distance learning might look like this:

- Level 1: Learning about social networks—definitions, history, background, and examples.
- Level 2: Designing for social networks—profiling, blogging, wiki-ing, and friending.

- Level 3: Studying social networks—ethics, uses, misuses, policing, and supporting.
- Level 4: Learning from and with social networks—social networks for teaching and learning, science, research, and theory building.

And finally, maybe we do not need to worry about solitary learners poised in front of a computer. Obviously they want friends, just as the child on the playground does. Virtual friends perhaps, but in many cases true friends. And, for all those social networkers out there, remember the old saying, "we are known by our friends!"

REFERENCES

Boyd, D. (2006, December 12). Friends, friendsters, and top 8: Writing community into being on social network sites. *First Monday, 11*(12). Retrieved from http://firstmonday.org/issues/issue11_12/boyd/index.html

Boyd, D., & Ellison, N. (2007). Social network sites: Definition, history, and scholarship. *Journal of Computer-Mediated Communication, 13*(1), article 11.

Sunden, J. (2003). *Material virtualities: Approaching online textual embodiment.* New York, NY: Peter Lang.

---

1 – LEARN ABOUT SOCIAL NETWORKING
2 – DESIGN FOR SOCIAL NETWORKS
3 – STUDY SOCIAL NETWORKS
4 – LEARN FROM AND WITH SOCIAL NETWORKS

Where Is as Important as Why, When, and What

Michael Simonson

Where? A home office? You bet! The solitary learner and solitary instructor need a place to learn or teach—a home office. The home office is a growth area of the 21st century—more are working from home, and many students are learning from home.

Just what constitutes a home office—is it the couch and 50-inch HDTV? Is it in the garage? Or, can it be my smartphone and the kitchen table. Well, none of these options are going to work, especially when most online courses are designed for the student to spend about 8 hours per week for each course they are taking at a distance. The home office, and home classroom should probably be a dedicated place—a place with "stuff."

Here is a list of what seems to be the consensus of what should be in the home office—the Big 20, if you would.

1. A modern computer with monitor
2. Software—MS Office at a minimum
3. A desk
4. A chair
5. Lighting—ceiling and desktop
6. A high speed internet connection—a cable modem, for example
7. A wireless router
8. Telephone with speaker and cordless handset
9. Electrical outlets with surge protectors
10. An all-in-one printer (copier, printer, fax, scanner)
11. Back-up drive
12. Uninterruptable power supply
13. File cabinet
14. Storage
15. Fire-proof safe
16. Paper shredder
17. USB webcam with built-in microphone
18. HDTV connected to cable
19. Supplies
20. Bookshelves

What a list, and oops, we forgot the most important item—a room with doors that can be closed. The distractions in the home are too powerful to be ignored; closed doors keep cats, kids, noise, and the home part of the home office outside.

And finally, as Theodore Roosevelt said, "When you play, play hard; when you work, don't play at all." So, when in your home office, don't play at all—or do the laundry.

RICHARD E. CLARK, EDITOR

LEARNING
From MEDIA

■ Arguments, Analysis, and Evidence, Second Edition ■

Foreword by Michael Simonson
Charles Schlosser and Michael Simonson, Series Editors
A VOLUME IN PERSPECTIVES IN INSTRUCTIONAL TECHNOLOGY AND DISTANCE LEARNING

Get Your Copy Today—Information Age Publishing

Distance Learning Leaders—Who Are They?

Michael Simonson

Recently, a program of study leading to a certificate as a distance learning leader was held at Nova Southeastern University. At the core of the 6-week long program was the definition offered of a leader.

A distance learning leader is a visionary capable of action who guides an organization's future, its vision, mission, goals, and objectives. The leader guides the organization and its people who have faith in the leader, and have a clear understanding and acceptance of the organization's worthwhile and shared vision and goals. A distance learning leader has competence in knowing, designing, managing, leading and visioning distance education.

The whole idea of training to develop leaders is an interesting one. The military trains its officers to be leaders during intensive sessions such as the U.S. Marine Corps' Basic School, a 6-month immersion in all that one could imagine for the new junior Marine officer. The Navy has the Surface Warfare Officers School in Newport, RI, which is a series of schools for officers of various ranks who attend several times during their naval careers. Without exception these schools are months long, and totally dominate the time and the of those in attendance. Then, we have West Point, Annapolis, and the Air Force Academy—certainly colleges, but also designed to produce military leaders.

Are we naïve to think we can prepare leaders of distance education organizations in 2 days and 6 weeks of online follow up? Or, are there a common core of skills, competencies, and ideas that can be taught, shared, and learned that will produce a new leader. Certainly the idea of certification programs to prepare leaders is becoming wide spread, and if the marketplace decides, then these many and varied programs must be doing something right. We at the *Distance Learning Magazine* would love to hear from our subscribers and readers about his topic—are leaders trained or do they emerge? Let us know your thoughts, and if you have specific insights or experiences, write an article.

And finally, as Walter Lippmann said "the final test of a leader is that [the leader leaves behind] in others the conviction and the will to carry on ... the genius of a good leader is to leave behind a situation which common sense, without the grace of genius, can deal with successfully." If distance education—distance teaching and distance learning—is to become mainstream, then many leaders in a multitude of locations will be needed. Informed leaders who believe in high quality and in the rigorous application of sound teaching principles to the learning process.

Distance Education

Statewide, Institutional, and International Applications

Readings From the Pages
of *Distance Learning* Journal

Compiled by Michael Simonson

A Volume in Perspectives
in Instructional Technology
and Distance Education

Get Your Copy Today—Information Age Publishing

Technology Plans and Distance Education

Michael Simonson

Most have heard about, and some have read, the U.S. Department of Education's National Educational Technology Plan, titled "Toward a New Golden Age In America Education" (http://www.ed.gov/about/offices/list/os/technology/plan/2004/plan.pdf). If you have not obtained a copy, you should. Actually, it is not bad reading.

One recurring theme of this plan is the importance today and in the future of distance education/e-learning/virtual schools. According to the report,

> About 25% of all K-12 public schools now offer some form of e-learning or virtual school instruction. Within the next decade every state and most schools will be doing so ... traditional schools are turning to distance education to expand offerings for students and increase professional development opportunities for teachers. (p. 34)

The report goes on to list and explain seven major recommendations. These seven are:

1. Strengthen leadership
2. Consider innovative budgeting
3. Improve teacher training
4. Support e-learning and virtual schools
5. Encourage broadband access
6. Move toward digital content
7. Integrate data systems

The plan's 46 pages are supplemented by lists of federal activities that support the use of technology in education.

It is interesting that this plan often identifies some aspect of distance education as critical to the future of education. Virtual schools are given special attention as important to the future of American education. It is also significant that the importance of leadership is stressed in the Plan and is the first of the seven recommendations. It is implied that, without enlightened leaders, effective technology implementation will not occur, and without technology schools will continue to fail.

The plan is a starting point. Schools and organizations might use the Plan as they develop their own strategy for encouraging e-learning and distance education. Certainly, more specifics and clear direction for implementation than found in the USDE Plan would be needed.

Distance education has become mainstream—widely practiced, generally understood, and critically important. Distance teaching and learning are innovations, even today, although these two components of distance education are soon to become regular and expected aspects of education. Our field must now live up to this long sought after importance.

And finally, in this era of grading and rating schools, it is obvious that the school that does not include instructional technology and distance education in its vision for the future and its planning for today is a school that is outdated and out of touch—a school that is failing.

EVERY EDUCATIONAL ORGANIZATION NEEDS AN INSTRUCTIONAL TECHNOLOGY AND DISTANCE EDUCATION PLAN.

Accreditation and Quality in Distance Education

Michael Simonson

In March of 2006, the U.S. Departmen of Education's Office of Postsecondary Education released an interesting report titled "Evidence of Quality in Distance Education Programs Drawn from Interviews with the Accreditation Community." What is interesting and important about this document is the approach used to collect information: 12 accrediting organizations were asked to identify representatives who had served on evaluation teams for schools offering distance education programs. These representatives were asked to identify "Good Practices and Red Flags." Their comments make great reading for anyone interested in identifying quality strategies for teaching and learning at a distance.

The report is organized into six sections, each dealing with various indicators of quality. The six are Mission, Curriculum, Faculty, Students, Sustainability, and Evaluation and Assessment. In each category are dozens of indicators of quality and red flags—danger signs that often indicate a weak or ineffective distance education program.

Some of the most interesting positive indicators are:

- The mission statement contains an explicit statement of the purpose of distance education;

- The regular faculty have oversight of the distance education curriculum;
- The regular faculty are actively involved in course design;
- There is a strong and active faculty development process;
- The university provides instructional design support for distance education;
- There is 24/7 technology support;
- There are academic advisers for distance education students;
- A systematic approach is applied to the growth and management of the distance education program
- There are clear plans for the future of distance education;
- Evaluation of distance education courses and programs are used for continuous improvement; and
- Input from faculty and students is used for program improvement.

Of equal interest and importance are some of the most noteworthy "red flags."

- There are two separate approaches, even mission statements for traditional and distance education;
- There are two target populations for traditional and distance education;

- There are two course approval processes for traditional and distance education;
- Distance education courses are designed using a "cookie-cutter" approach;
- Faculty attempt or are encouraged to directly convert traditional courses to distance delivered courses;
- There are two course evaluation systems, one for traditional and one for distance education;
- Some student services must be accessed face-to-face by distant students;
- Distant students are often confused about contact people at the institution;
- The institution has a history of started and stopped distance education programs;
- Few, other than administrators, know about the institution's distance education program;
- There are a large number of distant students who drop out; and
- There are many complaints from distant students.

Obviously, it is important to read the report to clearly understand these two lists. The report also contains many other comments of the accrediting agency representatives. And, distance education can not be improved merely by using checklists. However, this report by the U.S. Department of Education is must reading for those dedicated to quality teaching and learning at a distance.

And finally, it is certainly a positive sign that so many organizations are offering suggestions, most based on research, not opinion, about improving quality in distance education—reports designed to produce quality without mandates, effectiveness without edicts, and performance without prescriptions.

REFERENCE

U. S. Department of Education. (2006). *Evidence of quality in distance education programs drawn from interviews with the accreditation community.* Retrieved April 30, 2007, from http://www.itcnetwork.org/AccreditationEvidenceofQualityinDEPrograms.pdf

If it Is Intellectual, Can it Be Property?

Michael Simonson

Carol Twigg, executive director of the Center for Academic Transformation, has written and spoken extensively in the area of intellectual property and ownership of online courses and course materials. A reading of the abstract of her excellent monograph *Intellectual Property Policies for a New Learning Environment* is a requirement for any serious distance educator (Twigg, 2000). It is well-written, informative, and thought-provoking.

Reading Twigg's monograph got me to thinking about the two words—intellectual and property. Intellectual has a number of definitions, but most deal with the idea of the use of the intellect, and the showing or possessing of intelligence. Intellect, by the way, is the power of knowing and understanding. Property, on the other hand, refers to things that are owned or possessed. Usually property means things like land or objects that a person legally owns. So, intellectual property is "intelligence that is legally owned." Or, is it?

The source of the millennium, the wikipedia (can you believe doctoral students are citing the wikipedia? Go figure!), defines intellectual property (IP) as:

> a legal entitlement which sometimes attaches to the expressed form of an idea, or to some other intangible subject matter. This legal entitlement generally enables its holder to exercise exclusive rights of use in relation to the subject matter of the IP. The term intellectual property reflects the idea that this subject matter is the product of the mind or the intellect, and that IP rights may be protected at law in the same way as any other form of property.

Somehow, the wikipedia definition seems different than what is meant when the two words are defined separately.

Twigg writes eloquently about course and course materials ownership, and draws several conclusions. Of the most interesting is the statement that "there is a radically different—and infinitely simpler—solution if we treat the intellectual property issue not as a legal issue but as an academic issue" (p. 29). The question of ownership becomes less contentious and more collegial when the rights of faculty and institutions are satisfied equally.

And finally, Seneca probably had it right 2,000 years ago when he said, "The best ideas are common property."

REFERENCE

Twigg, C. (2000). *Intellectual property policies for a new learning environment.* Retrieved February 25, 2006, from http://www.center.rpi.edu/PewSym/mono2.html

It Costs How Much?

Estimating the Costs to Design and Develop a Distance Delivered Course

Michael Simonson

Course design and development is a basic process traditionally accomplished by a teacher, professor, or trainer, often with the assistance of an instructional developer and sometimes with the use of production specialists such as graphic artists, videographers, and computer programmers.

Face-to-face classes are most often designed by the teacher or trainer who is also the instructor. As a matter of fact, most educators consider the design and development of courses to be their responsibility, and often claim that courses they produce are their intellectual property.

The popularization of distance education has begun to change the traditional and largely private course design and development environment. With the advent of hybrid courses taught partially at a distance and partially face-to-face, and online courses taught almost totally at a distance, the design and development of courses has become more visible and costs have come under greater scrutiny.

The Sloan Foundation has defined online instruction as having at least 80% of the course content delivered online (Allen & Seaman, 2005). An online course is taught by an instructor who delivers the content and interacts with students.

Estimating the cost for the design and development of an online course is little discussed in the literature of distance education. One exception is a short paper by Hartnett (2002), who describes various processes for estimating the cost for the design and development of custom courses. Hartnett recommends estimating the costs for design and development using several approaches, then making a subjective decision.

Method 1: Best Estimate Method. This method estimates costs by trying to determine how long the project will take, including the work of anyone involved, and multiplying the number of hours by a pre-determined hourly rate.

Method 2: Screen (page) Count Method. This method estimates the number of computer screens or content pages an online course would have and multiplying that by $200-$500 per screen page, depending on the complexity of the information displayed.

Usually, a one hour lesson led by an instructor would use 3-5 screens or pages of content. These 3-5 screens or pages would make up a major topic in a course. Simonson, Smaldino, Albright, and Zvacek (2006) have described a model for organizing distance education courses that uses the topic as the basic building block. Topics are combined to make modules, and modules are combined with complementary modules to make units of instruction. The Unit-Module-Topic (UMT) model is becoming widely used by course designers (Simonson, 2006).

Method 3: Seat Time Method. Probably the oldest method is to estimate student seat time and multiply that times a predetermined cost, often up to $25,000 for one hour of instruction. This amount is the often quoted, if little used, industry standard.

Method 4: Comparative Project Method. For this method, the costs for developing a new course are compared to the costs for developing a similar, previously developed course, where costs were carefully recorded.

Method 5: Time Feel Method. For this method, the amount of time that is needed to complete a course is estimated to determine the number of hours needed to complete the design and development; this number is then multiplied by the going rate for those involved in the process.

Obviously, these methods involve a considerable amount of subjectivity. Two examples are provided next to clarify how costs are often estimated.

Example 1: A Comparative Project Method. At a recent convention of the Iowa Distance Learning Association, Bowers (2006) described the costs for outsourcing the design and development of courses for an extensive online program. Bowers identified these out-of-pocket costs for the design and development of an online course:

- Course Development Fee = $2,400
- Peer Reviewer Fee = $600
- Clerical Staff Support = $1,500

- Instructional Design and Media Development (Embanet.com) = ~13,500

Estimated Total Cost = ~$16,000

This cost did not include the costs associated with the staff that supervised and coordinated the design and development process.

Example 2: Estimating Using the Best Estimate and Screen Count Methods. The typical three-credit college level course has somewhere between 12 and 15 modules. A module is usually a week of instruction that typically would have 3 hours of content presentation, which means there would be at least 36 hours of content instruction during a semester (A rule of thumb is that for each hour of content instruction or delivery, students will spend about 2 hours outside of class studying, preparing, or completing assignments).

Most often, a professor, instructor, or teacher has already collected the content materials for a course: the lectures, videos, audios, PowerPoints, and other learning experiences.

A. **Best Estimate Method—**

- Overload to Instructor: $3,500
- Course Design, Subject Matter Expert: ~200 hours @ ~$60/hour = $12,000
- Production Costs: ~200 hours@ ~$40/hour = $8,000
- Production Materials: ~$1,000
- Indirect Costs: ~ 40% =$9,800

Total Best Estimate for 12 Module, 3 Credit Course = $34,300

B. **Screen Count Method—**

- ~3 screens/pages of instruction per topic
- ~5 topics/module
- 12 modules/3-credit course = ~180 screens/pages of instruction @ ~$250/page =

Total Screen Count Estimate for 12 Module, 3 Credit Course = $45,000

These two methods for estimating the cost for designing a 3-credit online course give a cost estimate range somewhere between $34,300 and $45,000.

And finally, accurately determining the cost for developing an online course is a subjective activity. Costs "depend," and many consider cost information proprietary. Quality instruction is expensive. Let us not kid ourselves. Whether costs are easily identifiable, or hidden within existing personnel budgets, the design of an effective online course requires talent, skill, and preparation, all of which mean "money."

REFERENCES

Allen, I., & Seaman, J. (2005). *Growing by degrees: Online Education in the United States, 2005.* Wellesley, MA: Babson College.

Bowers, P. (2006). *Designing online courses: A team-based, instructional design model.* Cedar Rapids, IA: Iowa Distance Learning Association.

Hartnett, J. (2002). Pricing secrets revealed: An insider's perspective on how custom course are priced. *Online Learning, 6*(3), 24-26.

Simonson, M., Smaldino, S., Albright, M., & Zvacek, S. (2006). *Teaching and learning at a distance: Foundations of distance education.* Upper Saddle River, NJ: Prentice-Hall.

$34,000–$45,000 PER COURSE.

Volume 15, Number 4, 2014

Quarterly Review
OF Distance
Education

RESEARCH THAT GUIDES PRACTICE

Editors:
Michael Simonson
Charles Schlosser

≡IAP
INFORMATION AGE
PUBLISHING

An Official Journal of the
Association for Educational Communications and Technology

QUARTERLY REVIEW OF DISTANCE EDUCATION,
SUBSCRIBE TODAY!
WWW.INFOAGEPUB.COM

MOOC Madness

Michael Simonson

"Though this be madness, yet there is method in't"

—Hamlet, Act II, Scene ii, line 211, Shakespeare

Massive open online courses, or MOOCs, pronounced interestingly enough as moooooks as in cow sounds, are the "talk of the town." The October 5, 2012 Section B of *The Chronicle of Higher Education* dedicated its entire issue to the topic of MOOCs. The *New York Times* has written about MOOCs, and even South Florida's own *Sun Sentinel* has opined on the topic of MOOCS.

Just what are MOOCs and what do they offer to the field of distance education? Simply, the name tells it all. MOOC courses are massive, often with enrollments in the tens of thousands. Next, they are open, meaning open access courseware is used to deliver the course, and enrollment is open to anyone who is interested. Next, MOOCs are online, fully online and asynchronous. And last, they are courses, often a digitized version of a traditional lecture class with sessions recorded in video, audio, and posted online.

But, are MOOCs distance education, as many think? First, one needs to define distance education. *Distance Learning* journal has regularly applied this definition: "Institutionally-based formal education, where the learning group is separated, and where interactive communications technologies are used to connect the instructor, learners

and resources" (Simonson, Smaldino, Albright, & Zvacek, 2012).

At first glance this definition does seem to include MOOCs as they are most often configured. MOOCs are institutionally-based; at least originally they were. The great universities of the United States, such as the Massachusetts Institute of Technology, and Stanford, offer MOOCs. Interestingly, many of the instigators of MOOCs initiatives have left their universities to offer massive online courses via private corporations.

Next, it is obvious that the learning group is separated; at least the learners and resources are geographically separated. But what about the instructors? Certainly MOOC designers and the talent featured in the videos can be considered instructors, but are these individuals actually involved in the use of the MOOC or are they "just talent?" Instructor involvement in the teaching and learning process is unclear.

Most definitely, communications technologies are used to deliver content and make the content available to learners; most often content is digitized content via the Web. Often, class presentations are video recorded, documents are digitized, and self-test quizzes and exams are written and programmed, often with self-scoring. Great stuff, but ...?

So, are MOOCs distance education? A closer examination of the definition of distance education may be helpful. Distance education consists of distance teaching AND distance learning—two components of the education process. Do MOOCs provide both teaching and learning? Some say no, since the instructional aspects of MOOCs are programmed and offered but only as a prepackaged self-study system.

MOOCs are usually loaded with outstanding content, and well-delivered presentations, but those who would claim that MOOCs are the future of higher education need only review the instructional films and instructional video phenomena of the 1960s and 1970s. Excellent self-study, but not education.

And finally, there is much to be learned from the study of MOOCs. As Shakespeare wrote in Hamlet, "there is method in't."

REFERENCES

Shakespeare, W. *Hamlet*, Act II, Scene ii, line 211

Simonson, M., Smaldino, S., Albright, M., & Zvacek, S. (2012). *Teaching and learning at a distance: Foundations of distance Education* (5th ed.). Boston, MA: Pearson.

MOOCs = EXCELLENT SELF STUDY, BUT NOT EDUCATION.

Apps
The 3 Rs and the 3 Ps

Michael Simonson

As with any new instructional technology, there are those who claim the new tool or idea is going to revolutionize education, and smartphone and tablet applications ("apps") are new. However, a review of the thousands of apps available indicates that there are currently three viable categories for education. Let's call these categories the 3 Rs.

Remediation is the first category of smartphone applications. These apps are designed to reinforce skills or knowledge learned previously, but that need some refreshing or practice. Excellent examples of remediation apps are *Flashcards+* and *Cram*.

Reference applications allow the learner to look up basic information, like the definition of a word, or a date, or a fact. *National Geographic's World Atlas* and the *Miriam Webster Collegiate Dictionary* are "must have" reference apps.

Reminders are the "to do"-type applications, such as meeting reminders, homework dates, and locators. *Find iPhone* is a great reminder app because it reminds us of the location of an iPhone. Parents love this app because if you find the iPhone you usually will find the iPhone user.

Many distance educators are asked by colleagues and friends about the educational appropriateness of using smartphone apps. The 3 Ps help answer these types of questions.

The first P relates to Parental Control. Young children often benefit from educational apps, but for pre-teens it is recommended that parents install and supervise the apps that are on a smartphone. The second P, Parental Review, is aimed at learners in middle and high school. If a student has a smartphone it should be subject to periodic parental review. The final P, Parental Trust, means that the parent trusts the child to use the smartphone correctly.

Apps are tremendous resources, and like any resource there is a set of skills involved in their use. In schools, media specialists are experts in application appropriateness and use. Parents can ask them for app advice. Another way to identify educationally appropriate content is to seek apps that are linked to traditional, long-standing educational tools. For example, *Curious George* has been around a long time, and the *Curious George* app supports the program and is excellent.

For distance educators, the thoughtful use of apps is a great way to improve instruction and expand access—the course syllabus, e-learning lesson, and webinar session should have an app list to accompany the traditional reference list. However, we should not expect too much from apps; they are not replacements for teachers, nor should they be.

And finally, the fourth app R is Recreation—certainly an exciting use of the smartphone, *after* homework is finished.

Edited by Anymir Orellana, Terry L. Hudgins, & Michael Simonson

The Perfect Online Course

BEST PRACTICES FOR DESIGNING AND TEACHING

A Volume in
Perspectives in Instructional Technology
and Distance Education

Get Your Copy Today—Information Age Publishing

Ethics and Distance Education

Michael Simonson

Ethics—right and wrong! Most students think they are ethical, yet a very high number admit they have cheated. Most know that it is improper to copy the work of others, yet plagiarism is reported to be widespread. And, one often heard criticism of distance education is the fear that "it is too easy for students to cheat! How do you know who is taking the test?"

Ethical behavior has long been a concern of educators. The United States Bureau of Education published the "Cardinal Principles of Secondary Education" in 1928 in an attempt to clarify right and wrong in teaching and learning, and to promote ethical behavior. More recently, the Markkula Center for Applied Ethics at Santa Clara University (n.d.) has provided extensive information about ethical behavior and the meaning of right versus wrong.

As distance education has become a mainstream approach in schools and colleges, there has been an increased concern about cheating, plagiarism, disruptive behavior, respect of others, and proper use of resources—online and local. These concerns have generally not been faced head-on by distance education leaders. Rather, right and wrong behaviors have been delegated to the background, pushed aside by more exotic concepts such as bandwidth, learning management systems, and operating systems.

Studying ethics for most would require a return to college to attend one of the core classes in philosophy that used to be required of all students (but which apparently have been replaced more recently by classes in business—which may explain in part why ethical behavior of students is of such a concern to professors and teachers). At any rate, if distance education is to be accepted, and not just tolerated, it is important that rigorous, high-quality teaching and learning systems must be in place—and ethical behavior is at the core of rigor and quality.

Two options that promote ethical behavior, mutually supportive, might be considered by distance education leaders. First is the study of what is right and wrong when participating in online classes—a study of ethical behavior. A taxonomy of study includes:

1. knowledge of what is ethical and what is not;
2. understanding of proper actions of students; and
3. application of ethical behaviors to the teaching and learning process.

Next, distance education policy manuals should include sections dealing with ethical behavior, including:

1. development of an institutional code of ethical behavior;
2. explanation of student responsibilities related to the categories of unethical behavior, including:
   • plagiarism,
   • cheating,
   • disruptive behaviors, and
   • deceptive actions;
3. establishment of a process of enforcement, including sanctions for violations of ethical behavior; and
4. implementation of training and remediation systems for instructors and students.

While it is unclear if cheating and plagiarism are more widespread in online courses than traditional ones, it is obvious that the perception held by many is that distance education courses and programs seem more likely to provide opportunities for unethical behavior. Distance educators should face this issue head-on.

And finally, as Proust said centuries ago, when "we cheat other people, we exist alone."

REFERENCES

Bureau of Education. (1928). *Cardinal principles of secondary education* (Bulletin, 1918, No. 35). Washington, DC: U.S. Government Printing Office.

Santa Clara University. (n.d.). *What is ethics?* Retrieved from http://www.scu.edu/ethics/practicing/decision/whatisethics.html

Britannica (Not Wikipedia)

Michael Simonson

Wikipedia begins its explanation of the Encyclopaedia Britannica by saying:

The Encyclopædia Britannica is a general English-language encyclopaedia published by Encyclopædia Britannica, Inc., a privately-held company. The articles in the Britannica are aimed at educated adult readers, and written by a staff of about 100 full-time editors and over 4,000 expert contributors. It is widely regarded as the most scholarly of encyclopaedias.

The Encyclopedia Britannica says this about Wikipedia:

free, Internet-based encyclopaedia operating under an open-source management style. It is overseen by the nonprofit Wikimedia Foundation ... a troubling difference between Wikipedia and other encyclopaedias lies in the absence of editors and authors who will accept responsibility for the accuracy and quality of their articles. These observers point out that identifiable individuals are far easier to hold accountable for mistakes, bias, and bad writing than is a community of anonymous volunteers, but other observers respond that it is not entirely clear if there is a substantial difference. Regardless of such controversies—perhaps in part because of them—Wikipedia has become a model of what the collaborative Internet community can and cannot do.

Certainly, even today in the age of googling and social networking, the Encyclopaedia Britannica is considered to be one of the most prestigious references and resources for general information about almost any topic. Reviewers claim that the Britannica covers "all human knowledge."

Until recently "all human knowledge" did not include distance education; now it does. In the *2009 Encyclopaedia Britannica Book of the Year,* distance education/learning is explained and defined (in the past tense, by the way) on page 231.

Four characteristics distinguished distance education. First, distance education was by definition carried out through institutions; it was not self-study or a nonacademic learning environment. The institutions might or might not offer traditional classroom-based instruction as well, but they were eligible for accreditation by the same agencies as those employing traditional methods.

Second, geographic separation was inherent in distance learning, and time might also separate students and teachers. Accessibility and convenience were important advantages of this mode of education. Well-designed programs could also bridge intellectual, cultural, and social differences between students.

Third, interactive telecommunications connected the learning group with each other and with the teacher. Most often, electronic communications, such as email, were used, but traditional forms of communication, such as the postal system, might also play a role. Whatever the medium, interaction was essential to distance education, as it was to any education. The connections of learners, teachers, and instructional resources became less dependent on physical proximity as communications systems became more sophisticated and widely available; consequently, the Internet, cell phones, and e-mail had contributed to the rapid growth in distance education.

Finally, distance education, like any education, established a learning group, sometimes called a learning community, which was composed of students, a teacher, and instructional resources—i.e., the books, sound, video, and graphic displays that allowed the student to access the content of instruction."

And finally, legitimization of distance education/ learning must continue to be a goal of professionals in the field, and the Encyclopaedia Britannica has now made that a little easier.

REFERENCE

Simonson, M. (2009). Distance learning. In *The 2009 book of the year* (p. 231). Chicago: Encyclopaedia Britannica.

Educational Colonialism

Michael Simonson

Colonialism is the policy or practice of acquiring full or partial political control over another country, occupying it with settlers, and exploiting it economically. Education is the process of receiving or giving systematic, formal instruction, usually at a school or university—also, an enlightening experience involving teaching and learning.

So, is there such a thing as educational colonialism, which could be defined as the policy of acquiring full or partial control over another country's educational system, occupying it with nonlocal teachers, and exploiting it educationally?

Distance education may be an example of educational colonialism, as the practice of teaching and learning at a distance seems to be the antithesis of local education. Yet, most readers of this journal probably think it may be possible to combine the advantages of distance education with local control of schools, colleges and universities.

The massive open online course is a notable application of distance education. MOOCs utilize the expertise of eminent scholars and teachers, often from the most prestigious universities, to offer world-class education to anyone in the world, sometimes for free.

Is it possible for the field of distance education to be tailored to meet local needs? Can distance education, defined as "institutionally based formal education with interactive telecommunications systems used to connect learners, instructors, and resources" (Schlosser & Simonson, 2009, p. 1) be community, region, or state based? Or, must distance education ultimately be a massive system?

Possibly we should be advocating a new approach to distance education—the localization of distance education. For that, another definition—of localization or local control—is needed. Here is what the Great Schools Partnership (2013) says about local control in education:

> In education, local control refers to (1) the governing and management of public schools by elected or appointed representatives serving on governing bodies, such as school boards or school committees, that are located in the communities served by the schools, and (2) the degree to which local leaders, institutions, and governing bodies can make independent or autonomous decisions about the governance and operation of public schools. (para. 1)

The concept of local control is grounded in a philosophy of government premised on the belief that the individuals and institutions closest to the students and most knowledgeable about a school—and most invested in the welfare and success of its educators, students, and communities—are best suited to making important decisions related to its operation, leadership, staffing, academics, teaching, and improvement.

Wow, an interesting situation. Distance education provides the promise of teaching and learning from the best people and places to nearly anyone, anywhere. Yet, there is considerable and important relevance to the local control of education, especially in the United States. Is localized distance education possible? Perhaps it is a topic worthy of study.

And finally, as Thomas Jefferson is purported to have said, perhaps written, "an educated citizenry is a vital requisite for our survival as a free people."

REFERENCES

Great Schools Partnership. (2013). Local control. Retrieved from the glossary of education reform website: http://edglossary.org/local-control/

Schlosser, L. A., & Simonson. (2009). *Distance education: Definition and glossary of terms* (3rd ed.). Charlotte, NC: Information Age.

LOCALIZATION OF DISTANCE EDUCATION—A TOPIC WORTHY OF STUDY.

Hooray!
Or, Here We Go Again!

Michael Simonson

Evaluation of Evidence-Based Practices in Online Learning: A Meta-Analysis and Review of Online Learning Studies is must reading for anyone involved in education generally, and distance education specifically. This report is a comprehensive review of 51 studies that:

- "contrasted an online to a face-to-face condition,
- measured student learning outcomes,
- used a rigorous research design, and
- provided adequate information to calculate an effect size." (p. ix)

The report's most quoted conclusion is printed in italics in its abstract and states, *"The meta-analysis found that, on average, students in online learning conditions performed better than those receiving face-to-face instruction"* (p. ix).

The 70-page report is well-written, informative, and scholarly. It is an important document that attempts to provide a state-of-the-research report on the effectiveness of online/distance education. Unfortunately, unless carefully read, the report can be misleading.

On page 51, the report's authors, staffers from SRI International's Center for Technology in Learning under contract to the U.S. Department of Education, clearly state what *should be* the most quoted outcome of this meta-analysis:

> Clark (1983) has cautioned against interpreting studies of instruction in different media as demonstrating an effect for a given medium inasmuch as conditions may vary with respect to a whole set of instructor and content variables. That caution applies well to the findings of this meta-analysis, which should not be construed as demonstrating that online learning is superior as a medium. Rather, it is the combination of elements in the treatment conditions, which are likely to include additional learning time and materials as well as additional opportunities for collaboration that has proven effective. (p. 51)

Learning time, materials and collaboration—the big 3. Apparently online students spent more time, had access to more materials, and collaborated differently than did the traditionally taught comparison students. No wonder online students tended to achieve better.

What we do not know from this report is *why* some students spent more time, accessed different materials, and had more collaboration opportunities. It is somewhat unfortunate that these important outcomes were not stressed instead of the misleading conclusion that *"students in online learning conditions performed better."*

Many will remember the meta-analyses of the 1980s that also misled a generation of educators into thinking that computer-based instruction was superior to classroom instruction (Kulik, Bangert, & Williams, 1983; Kulik, Kulik, & Cohen, 1979, 1980). The "Kulik" studies, as they were called, concluded that students using computer-based-instruction achieved better than students who were traditionally taught. More critical analyses revealed that most of the studies included in the "Kulik" studies were methodologically flawed (Clark, 1983). Unfortunately, a whole generation of educators implemented computer-based instruction, and then waited for positive effects that never materialized.

Certainly, the USDE Report is important. It represents a review of the best studies available. The Study's authors made every attempt to be methodologically and conceptually rigorous. Perhaps the author of the abstract was a marketing adviser rather than a researcher. At any rate, this report should be read and analyzed by all distance educators.

And finally, as George Washington said over 230 years ago, "facts are stubborn things: and whatever may be our wishes, our inclinations, or the dictates of our passions, they cannot alter the state of facts and evidence."

REFERENCES

Clark, R. (1983). Reconsidering research on learning from media. *Review of Educational Research, 53*(4), 445-459.

Kulik, C., Bangert, R., & Williams, G. (1983). Effects of computer-based teaching on secondary school students. *Journal of Educational Psychology, 75,* 19-26.

Kulik, C., Kulik, J., & Cohen, P. (1979). Research on audio-tutorial instruction: A meta-analysis of comparative studies. *Research in Higher Education, 11*(4), 321-341.

Kulik, C., Kulik, J., & Cohen, P. (1980). Instructional technology and college teaching. *Teaching of Psychology, 7*(4), 199-205.

U.S. Department of Education, Office of Planning, Evaluation and Policy Development. *Evaluation of Evidence-Based Practices in Online Learning: A Meta-Analysis and Review of Online Learning Studies,* Washington, DC Retrieved from http://www.ed.gov/about/offices/list/opepd?ppss?reports.html

Distance Education as a Disruptive Technology

Michael Simonson

A disruptive technology or disruptive innovation is a technological innovation, product, or service that eventually overturns the existing dominant technology or product in the market. Disruptive innovations can be broadly classified into lower-end and new-market disruptive innovations. A new-market disruptive innovation is often aimed at nonconsumption, whereas a lower-end disruptive innovation is aimed at mainstream customers who were ignored by established companies. Sometimes, a disruptive technology comes to dominate an existing market by either filling a role in a new market that the older technology could not fill ... or by successively moving up-market through performance improvements until finally displacing the market incumbents....

By contrast, "sustaining technology or innovation" improves product performance of established products. Sustaining technologies are often incremental however they can also be radical or discontinuous. (as cited in Wikipedia, in Teets, 2002)

Thus, technological innovations might be categorized along a continuum, from sustaining to disruptive. In education, a sustaining technology might be a SmartBoard, which in most applications is a way to present information dynamically and efficiently—a sus-taining upgrade to the chalkboard and overhead projector.

As a matter of fact, most attempts to integrate instructional technology into the traditional classroom are examples of sus-taining technologies—computer data projectors, DVD players, e-books—all which "improve product performance of *established* products." Most integrated technologies sustain, and do not disrupt.

On the other hand, distance education is certainly not a sustaining technology. Rather, distance education, virtual schooling, and e-learning are disruptive. For example, distance education is aimed at students (older, working, remotely located learners) who are "ignored by established companies" (traditional schools). Distance education presents a different package of performance attributes that are not valued by existing customers. Distance education has come to "dominate ... by filling a role ... that the older technology could not fill."

Clayton Christensen (2003; Christensen, Anthony, & Roth, 2004) has written extensively about the concept of disruptive technologies. Christensen's work has been widely embraced in business. His work helps explain why some established industries fail, and others spring up, seemingly from nowhere. No better example is the personal computer. Not a single mini-computer manufacturer has been a successful manufacturer of personal computers; they did not see the power of the new technology until others had captured market share.

Similarly, most in education have ignored the potential of looking at the ideas behind Christensen's theory, and how disruptive technologies might transform education and training.

In Florida, there is a mandate that every public school district must establish a virtual K-8 and K-12 school (Simonson, 2008). Many have wondered why Florida legislators would pass such a sweeping law. Perhaps the answer is disruptive technology. Whatever the reason for Florida to establish virtual schools, it is clear that distance education and virtual schooling are disrupting traditional education, and this may be a good thing. It might be a good idea for educators to become more cognizant of Clayton Christensen's work, and

the power of disruptive technologies to change education.

And finally, Christensen likes to say that because of disruptive technologies these are "scary" times for managers in big companies. It is likely that because of distance education the next few years are going to be *very scary* for school superintendents, college presidents, and training directors.

REFERENCES

Christensen, C. M. (2003). *The innovator's dilemma: The revolutionary book that will change the way you do business.* New York, NY: Harper-Collins.

Christensen, C. M., Anthony, S. D., & Roth, E. A. (2004). *Seeing what's next.* Boston, MA: Harvard Business School Press.

Simonson, M. (2008). Virtual schools mandated. *Distance Learning,* 5(4), 84-83.

Teets, J. (2002). Disruptive technology defined. Retrieved from http://www.distechs.com/index.php?page=disruptive-technology-defined

E-Books
The Future?

Michael Simonson

"We will no longer publish printed books in the field of education, we will only publish e-books."
—Statement heard in the executive offices of a large international publisher.

"A house without books is like a room without windows."
—Horace Mann

"Many people, myself among them, feel better at the mere sight of a book."
—Jane Smiley

What is trending in distance education? E-books! E-books are being proclaimed by some as the next major consequence of the digital revolution. These "futurists" forecast that the printed book is destined to go the way of Super-8 film, VHS tapes, and floppy disks.

E-books, simply defined as electronic versions of printed books, offer the reader many advantages. Certainly, the electronic book, newspaper, journal, even comic book are here to stay. There are many obviously advantages of electronic publishing. Pastore (2010) listed the major advantages of e-books. Some of his more interesting claims are:

- E-books promote reading. People are spending more time in front of screens and less time in front of printed books.
- E-books are faster and cheaper to produce than paper books, and are often cheaper to buy.
- E-books are easily updateable.
- E-books are searchable.
- E-books are portable. The reader can carry an entire library.
- E-books defy time: they can be delivered almost instantly.
- E-books can be annotated without harming the original work.
- E-books make reading accessible to persons with disabilities. Text can be resized for the visually impaired. Screens can be lit for reading in the dark.
- E-books can be hyperlinked for easier access to additional information.
- E-books can read aloud to you.
- E-books defeat attempts at censorship.

So, educators generally, and distance educators specifically, are now faced with a decision—the e-book or the printed book? And, if a favorite text is only available electronically or only in print form, should this influence the adoption decision? Interestingly, some publishers indicate they will make the choice for us—the electronic text will be the only option.

Is this an important issue? When one thinks about either/or decisions distance educators make, the medium used for the delivery of the printed word does not seem to rise to the level of some other controversial decisions, such choosing between virtual vs. brick and mortar schools, or the issue of open vs. proprietary CMSs.

But, perhaps this apparently simple issue—offering books in *only* an electronic format, a decision being made by several large publishers—is an issue that may have greater implications than one might expect. Certainly, the advantages of e-books listed by Pastore are important, but why are some in our field left a little cold by the decision by publishers to only publish textbooks in an electronic format? What is lost compared to what is gained? Most teachers think textbook selection is an academic issue, as is the decision about content delivery, and that access to accurate information in books is fundamental.

Journal and book editors know that "content is king," and that journal articles and books are created by knowledgeable authors *who can write*. The control of content, which is routinely signed away by authors when they agree to have their ideas, scholarship, and creativity published, actually means that content is controlled by publishers. This is not news. Copyright release forms are a part of the publishing process.

But, books have always been relatively immune from exclusive ownership. When we buy a book it belongs to us. Public libraries have long offered near universal access, and our ever-diligent librarians and media specialists have long guaranteed access, often to the consternation of publishers.

Is there a problem if the contents of books are continuously controlled by publishers, with access made available, if at all, only for money? Hmm …. Somehow this seems wrong.

Distance Learning would like to publish articles dealing with the issue of e-books and their impact on teaching and learning.

And finally, as Thomas Jefferson said, "I cannot live without books."

REFERENCE

Pastore, M. (2010). *50 benefits of ebooks*. Ithaca, NY: Zorba.

Books, Real and Otherwise

Michael Simonson

Crated, carted, cast aside,
printed works have liquefied
in shocking bouts of bookicide.

The printing press is done, perhaps,
and publishers have (boom!) collapsed
to clicky gadgets, gizmos, apps.

Digital books are all the rage,
touchless paper, turnless page.

Stores are only cyber spaces,
cold, electric, faceless places.

Bookshops closed, bookshelves cleared,
paperbacks have disappeared.

The age of print has culminated,
finished, finis, terminated.

—Susan M. Ebbers

Most agree that a book is a series of printed pages, bound together on one side, and with a cover—something real and physical. Almost everyone knows what a book is, and what books are not. But, maybe it is not that simple. What about virtual books, electronic books, online books? Are they real? Are they books? Or, are they something else—written content? Some textbook publishers would have us think that the electronic book, the virtual book, the online book, are superior to physical books. They are cheaper, more readily accessible, and more modern. But, are they books?

One interesting discussion about books deals with the role the book plays in society. The bestselling book, *The Book Thief*, subtly supports the importance of books. Liesel Meminger is a foster child living in World War II-era Germany. She steals books, including one salvaged from a book burning. Leisel saved and cherished the book. Her book did not burn, and it was a real book.

The reader of *The Book Thief* is left with many conflicting images as the story unfolds, but one stands out; somehow the books that Liesel steals and the books she reads save her and give her life meaning. That may not be the message the Markus Zusak, the author, wants the reader to remember, but books and their impact are certainly central to the story of the book thief. Liesel would just be a lost and lonely girl if she did not have books.

What about today? All the rage today is the electronic book, one that exists on a server as a recorded file. Electronic books are a great addition to the options available to the reader, but should electronic books replace real ones?

The electronic book file cannot be read without a software package and without a device such as a tablet reader. And, according to some publishers, the electronic book is not owned by you; rather, it belongs to the publisher—who lets you read it for a price.

Why should distance educators be concerned with the status of the book? What difference does it make if we do not have real books, but only have electronic ones? After all, distance educators are in the business of virtual things. Yet, somehow the real book seems important, even critical. Distance learners should read books. Most definitely. But does it matter if the book to be read is only online?

Well, the decision to have real or electronic books is being made for us. One large publisher is no longer offering bound copies (books) of its education titles, only electronic ones stored on a company server that must be accessed using a propriety software reader, and readers only get to rent the electronic book for 6 months (or longer for a bit more money). Is this a good idea? Publishers have our best interest in mind, don't they?

A solution: do not adopt a book for your course that does not have the option of a physical book. Certainly, electronic versions of textbooks should be options, but physical books must be available.

And finally, let's stop bookicide, the 21st century equivalent of book burning.

REFERENCE

Ebbers, S. M. (2011, November 13). *The age of books* [poem]. Retrieved from http://vocablog-plc.blogspot.com/2011/11/rise-of-digital-dictionaries-novels.html?utm_source=BP_recent&utm-medium=gadget&utm_campaign=bp_recent

Finding Maturity?

Michael Simonson

Maturity means growing up, getting older, settling in, and fully developing. Is distance education mature? Some think that a being mature means you can do what you want; others think it means doing what we should. Age does not determine maturity; maturity is knowing limitations and making the best of things. Is distance education a mature field, or is the field in its teen years—thinking mature but acting adolescent.

And finally, growing up still means you can have fun, and even be silly.

CPSIA information can be obtained at www.ICGtesting.com
Printed in the USA
LVOW09s0952160415

434745LV00006B/16/P